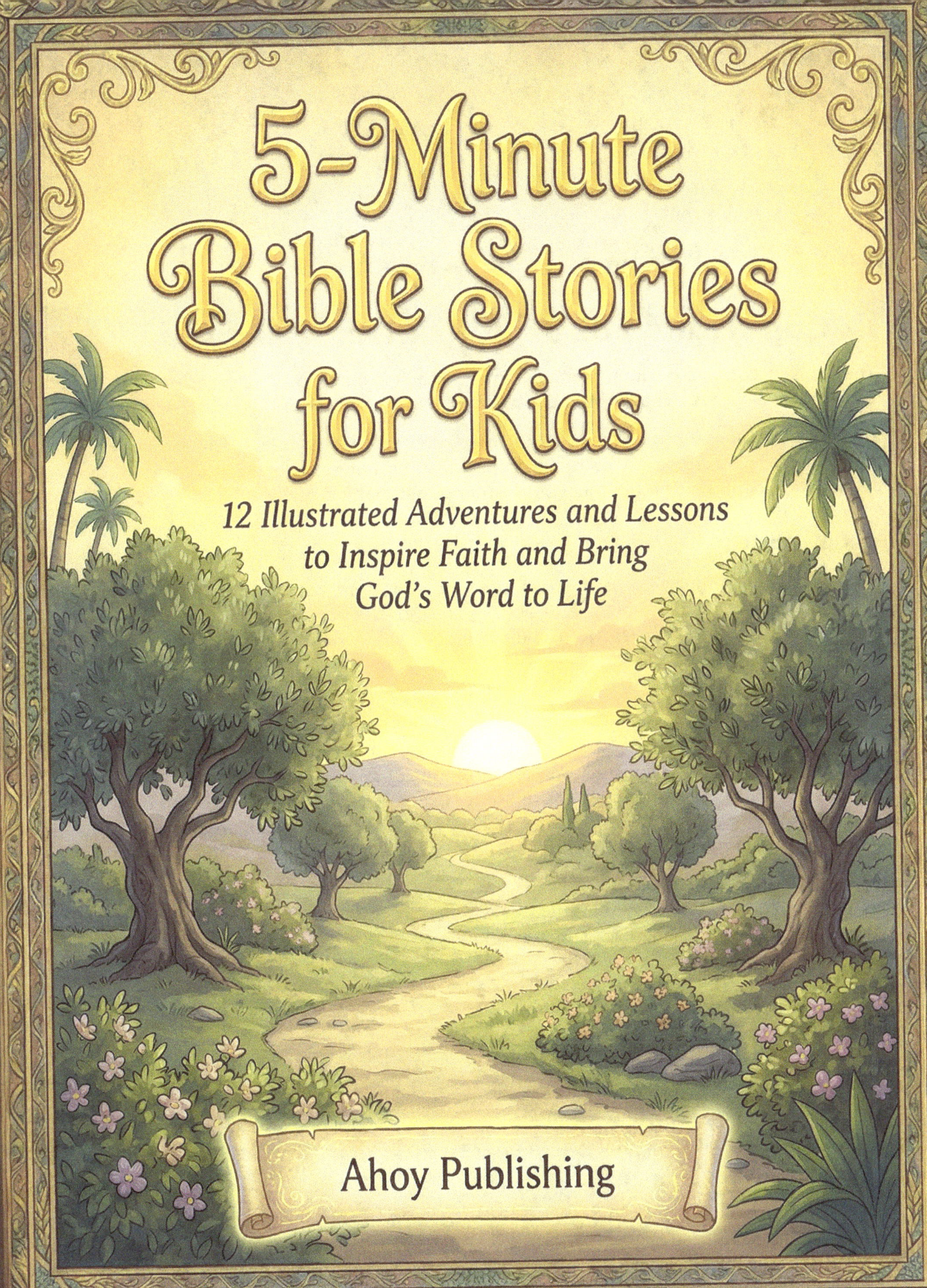

5-Minute
Bible Stories
for Kids
12 Illustrated Adventures and Lessons
to Inspire Faith and Bring
God's Word to Life
Ahoy Publishing

Keep the Conversation Going!

Download Your Free 'Little Hearts' Companion Pack

Thank you for sharing these stories with your little ones. We believe that the best part of a Bible story isn't just the reading— it's the connection that happens afterward. To help you bridge the gap between storytime and daily life, we've created a special collection of printable resources for your family.

- **Scripture Memory Cards:** 10 beautifully designed cards to help your child carry God's Word in their heart throughout the day. Perfect for the fridge, the car, or bedside.

- **The "Table Talk" Discussion Guide:** Simple, thoughtful questions for every story in this book. These prompts are designed to spark big conversations and help children see how God is working in their own lives.

- **"My Daily Conversation" Prayer Journal:** A gentle, two-page template that teaches children the habit of prayer through gratitude, reflection, and big dreams.

These resources are designed to turn five minutes of reading into a lifetime of faith. They are quick to print, easy to use, and crafted to help your child feel confident in God's love.

Scan the QR code below to download your free Activity Pack instantly!

Table of Contents

Welcome to Your Bible Adventure!

You're about to go on an amazing adventure. A journey through the most wonderful stories ever told. These stories come from the Bible, God's true Word that inspires hope and faith. They're filled with brave people, big surprises, and beautiful lessons that show us how much God loves us.

In this book, you'll meet:
- A tiny baby floating in a basket.
- A little boy who faced a giant.
- A man swallowed by a big fish.
- And a Savior named Jesus who came to change the world with His love.

Every story takes about five minutes to read, just the right size for your bedtime or story time. So, curl up, get cozy, and let's step into God's big story.

God Made Everything

Lesson: God made you, me, and all we see, and He said it was good.

(Based on Genesis 1)

In the beginning, there was... nothing.

No sun.

No stars.

No sky.

No sea.

No trees or animals.

"Let there be light!"

Just like that, light burst into the world, bright and beautiful, like someone turning on a warm, glowing lamp in a quiet room. Light flooded across the darkness. It filled every corner with color and warmth.

God gave the light a name: **Day.** And He gave the darkness a name: **Night.** Then God smiled and said, "This is good."

Next, God made the **sky.** It was big, wide, and blue, stretching over the earth like a soft, peaceful blanket. Clouds floated through it like cotton balls. The air swirled gently around the land.

And God said, **"This is good."**

Then came **land and sea.** God spoke, and the waters gathered into oceans and rivers. Dry land rose up, with mountains, valleys, beaches and cliffs.

On the land, **green grass** grew soft and thick. **Tall trees** stretched their arms toward the sky. **Tiny flowers** peeked from the dirt, opening their colorful faces to the new sun. God filled the land with every kind of plant. Some to eat, some to smell, and some just to look at and say, "Wow!"

And again, God said, **"This is good."**

Then God made two great lights in the sky. **The sun** to shine brightly during the day, warming the earth and making plants grow. **The moon** to glow softly at night, giving a gentle light to the world when the sun was sleeping. He scattered **millions of stars** across the night sky.

God looked at the sun, the moon, and the stars twinkling in the dark, and He said, **"This is good."**

Next, God filled the oceans with living creatures. **Big fish, tiny fish, slow-moving turtles,** and **flippy, floppy dolphins.**

Some creatures swam gracefully. Some wiggled and jiggled in funny ways. Some glowed deep in the darkest parts of the sea.

Then God filled the sky with **birds**. Soaring eagles, colorful parrots and sweet little sparrows flew across the sky. Birds chirped, sang, and flapped their wings with joy.

God said again, **"This is good."**

Slow turtles crawling along the ground. **Fast cheetahs** racing through tall grasses. **Tall giraffes** stretching their necks to munch on leaves high in the trees. **Tiny bugs** buzzing busily from flower to flower. **Furry bears** lumbering through the forest. **Soft bunnies** hopping across fields.

Each animal was unique. Each one was loved. And God said, **"This is good."**

But God wasn't finished yet. He had saved His **most special creation** for last.

God made **people**. A boy and a girl. He made them to smile, laugh, think, love, create, and care. He made them to enjoy the beautiful world He had made.

But even more, He made them to know Him, to walk with Him, to be His friends. He gave them His own breath of life. He made them in His own image.

When God looked at the boy and the girl, and at everything He had created, He said something even better:
"This is very good."

Then, God rested. Not because He was tired - God never gets tired! But because His beautiful, wonderful, perfect world was ready.

The oceans danced with life. The sky sang with light. The land burst with color and sound and joy. It was a masterpiece, made with love.

And do you know the best part? **You are part of God's plan too.** You were made by God's hands, with purpose and love.

Every time you see a star twinkle, a flower bloom, or a bird soar through the sky, remember: God made this world, and He made you too!

Little Prayer

Dear God, thank You for making the world and for making me. Help me take care of the things You made. Amen.

Noah Builds a Boat

Lesson: Even when others laugh, God sees your heart.

(Based on Genesis 6–9)

A long, long time ago, the world was a sad place. People had forgotten about God. They did whatever they wanted. They hurt each other with their words and their hands. They didn't care about right or wrong. Their hearts were full of selfishness, anger, and meanness.

It made God very sad. He had made the world so beautiful. He had filled it with love and light and goodness. But now, almost everyone had turned away from Him.

Almost everyone. There was one man who was different. His name was **Noah.** Noah loved God. He listened to God. He tried to do what was right, even when the people around him did wrong. God looked at Noah's heart and smiled.

He told Noah something important—something that would change everything. **"Noah,"** God said, "I am going to send a flood to wash away the badness. But I want to keep you and your family safe. **Build a big boat!"**

God gave Noah the instructions: Make it long, tall and strong, with enough room inside for animals and food. Noah had never built anything like that before. He didn't know how a flood could cover the whole earth. He had never seen rain like that. The sky was clear. The sun was shining.

But Noah didn't argue. He didn't say, "That's too hard!" or "That sounds crazy!" He trusted God.

So Noah got to work. He hammered. He sawed. He lifted heavy boards. He built the giant boat exactly the way God told him to.

As he worked, people walked by. They laughed at him. They pointed and made fun of him. **"Why build a boat in the middle of dry land?"** they said. **"There's no water here, silly Noah!"**

But Noah didn't stop. He kept building. Because **Noah believed God's words more than people's laughter.**

When the boat was ready, something amazing happened.

God sent two animals of every kind to Noah. Two **elephants** with big floppy ears. Two **lions** with fluffy manes. Two **turtles** with slow, steady steps. Two **rabbits** with twitchy noses.

Animals of **every color, size and shape!** Noah didn't have to chase them. God brought them to the ark.

Noah, his wife, his three sons, and their wives all got on the boat too. Then God did something wonderful.

God shut the door. And just in time.

Soon, dark clouds filled the sky. The wind blew harder and harder. And the rain started to fall. It wasn't just a little sprinkle. It poured and poured and poured. The ground turned into **rushing rivers.** The rivers turned into **wide oceans.**

The boat rocked gently on the water, floating safely above the deep flood. Noah, his family and all the animals were safe inside because they had obeyed God.

It rained for forty days and forty nights. The rain never stopped, not even once. Then, finally, the rain ended. The waters slowly went down.

Little by little, the boat rested **on top of a tall mountain.** Noah waited patiently inside the ark.

He sent out a dove to see if it could find dry land. When the dove didn't come back, Noah knew it was time.

Finally, one day, God spoke again: **"Come out of the boat."**

Noah and his family stepped onto dry land. The air smelled fresh and clean. The world looked new and bright, washed clean by God's hand.

Right there, Noah built an altar. He gave thanks to God with all his heart. And God made a promise, a **covenant**. He put a rainbow in the sky, bright, colorful and beautiful as a sign of His love.

God said, **"I will never flood the whole earth again. This is My promise to you."**

Whenever you see a rainbow stretched across the sky, you can remember: **God keeps His promises. And He sees the hearts of those who love and trust Him, just like He saw Noah.**

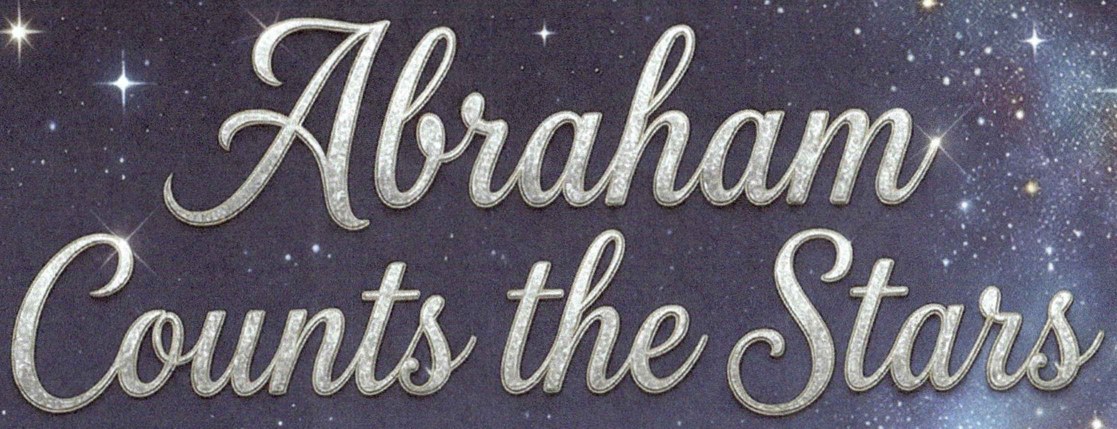

Abraham Counts the Stars

Lesson: If God makes a promise, He will keep it.

(Based on Genesis 15)

Long ago, there lived a man named **Abram.** Abram loved God with all his heart. He listened carefully when God spoke. He followed whenever God led.

One day, God made Abram a wonderful promise. God said, **"Abram, leave your home and your land. Go to a new place that I will show you. I will bless you. I will make your family so big that you won't even be able to count them!"**

Abram trusted God, even though he didn't know exactly where he was going. He packed up everything he owned. He loaded camels and donkeys. He rolled up his tents and cooking pots. He gathered his servants and flocks. He took his wife, **Sarai**, by the hand. And they started walking.

They traveled over hot, dusty deserts. They climbed rocky hills that scraped their sandals. They crossed wide rivers, their feet slipping on smooth stones. It wasn't easy. It wasn't fast. Sometimes, it was hot and hard. Sometimes, the nights were long and cold.

But Abram kept trusting God's promise. Everywhere they went, Abram built an altar. He stacked stones into a small tower and thanked God for leading him, step by step.

Days turned into months. Months turned into years. Abram and Sarai grew older, older than most grandmas and grandpas you know! And still... no children. No tiny feet padding through the tents. No giggles at bedtime. No lullabies in the evening. No little voices calling out, **"Daddy!"** or **"Mommy!"**

Sometimes, when Abram watched the other families laugh and play, his heart felt heavy and sad.

He wondered, **"Did I hear God right? Did I understand His promise?"**

One night, after a long day of traveling, Abram sat alone outside his tent. The stars began to blink into the sky, one by one. He looked up at them and sighed.

He prayed, **"Lord, You gave me a promise. But I don't have even one child. How can my family grow big like You said?"**

God heard Abram's prayer. And God answered.

Gently, God led Abram out under the dark, velvet sky. It was silent, sparkling with a million stars.

God said, **"Abram, look up. Try to count them!"** and Abram tilted his head and pointed. One, two... ten, fifty... too many to count! The stars stretched across the sky like a river of light.

The longer Abram looked, the more he saw. Tiny ones and bright ones, all twinkling together like a celebration.

Then God smiled, **"That's how many people will come from you. Your family will be that big!"**

Abram stared in wonder. It seemed impossible, but he believed God. And because Abram trusted Him, God called him **righteous**, which is a big word meaning **"right with God."**

Even though it felt like waiting forever, **God kept His promise.** Later, God changed Abram's name to **Abraham**, which means **"Father of Many."**

And guess what? Abraham's family really did grow as big as the stars in the sky! His children, grandchildren, great-grandchildren, and many more generations filled the earth, just like God said.

And from Abraham's family, a special child was born: **Jesus.** Jesus came so that the whole world could be part of God's forever family.

And today, when you look up at the night sky and see those twinkling stars, you can remember something wonderful: **God's promises never fail.** His promises are always shining, just like the stars. And every twinkle you see is like a little whisper from God: **"I am faithful. I always keep My promises."**

Baby in the Basket
Lesson: God cares for you and has a plan for your life.
(Based on Exodus 2)
34

A long time ago, in the land of Egypt, there lived a mean king called **Pharaoh.**

Pharaoh didn't like the people of God, called the **Israelites.** He was afraid they were becoming too many and too strong. So he made a terrible rule: He said that all baby boys born to the Israelites must be taken away.

It was a sad and scary time. Everyone wondered: **"What can we do?"**

But even when things looked scary, **God was still in control.**

One day, a sweet little baby boy was born. His mother looked at him and saw how precious he was. She knew she had to protect him no matter what.

For three whole months, **she hid him.** She rocked him quietly in her arms. She sang to him in soft whispers. She tiptoed around the house so no one would hear his tiny cries.

But babies grow. Soon the little boy kicked harder. He giggled louder. He stretched his arms and made happy sounds. It became harder and harder to hide him. His mother knew she had to do something brave, something only a mother's love could dream up.

She made a special basket out of reeds.

She coated it with tar and sticky pitch so it would float and not sink.

Then she wrapped her tiny baby boy in a soft blanket. She kissed his forehead, whispered a prayer, and placed him gently inside the basket.

With tears in her eyes, she carried the basket to the **river.**

The water moved gently, whispering and swirling around the tall green reeds. She set the basket on the water, tucking it safely among the grasses where it would be hidden.

Nearby, her daughter **Miriam** stayed close, hiding and watching carefully. The basket floated softly back and forth. Safe in the hands of God.

Now, at just the right time, something amazing happened. Pharaoh's daughter, the princess of Egypt, came down to the river to take a bath. As she walked along the water's edge, she spotted something unusual among the reeds.

"What is that?" she asked, pointing.

She sent her servant to fetch the basket. When the princess opened the lid, she gasped! Inside was a tiny baby, wide-eyed, wiggly, and beautiful. The princess's heart melted with love.

"This must be one of the Hebrew babies," she said softly.

At just that moment, brave little Miriam stepped out from her hiding place. She smiled sweetly and said, **"Would you like me to find someone to take care of the baby for you?"**

The princess smiled back. **"Yes, please!"** she said.

So Miriam ran as fast as her legs could carry her, all the way home to get her mother! God had made a way.

The baby's mother got to take care of her own son, safe under the princess's protection. She could hold him, rock him, feed him, and love him, without fear.

When the little boy grew older, the princess adopted him as her own son. She named him **Moses**, because she had drawn him out of the water.

Moses would grow up to be a great leader for God's people. He would help free the Israelites from Pharaoh's cruel rule. He would talk to God face to face. He would lead his people through deserts and seas toward a land of promise. But first, Moses was just a tiny baby, floating safely in a basket.

Even then, God had a big, beautiful plan for him.

God was watching. God was guiding. God was loving.

And just like Moses, **God has a special plan for you too.**

Even when you feel small, God sees you. When life feels scary, God holds you close.

His plans are always perfectly good, just like His love.

Little Prayer

Dear God, thank You for taking care of me. Help
me trust Your plan, even when I don't understand it.
Amen.

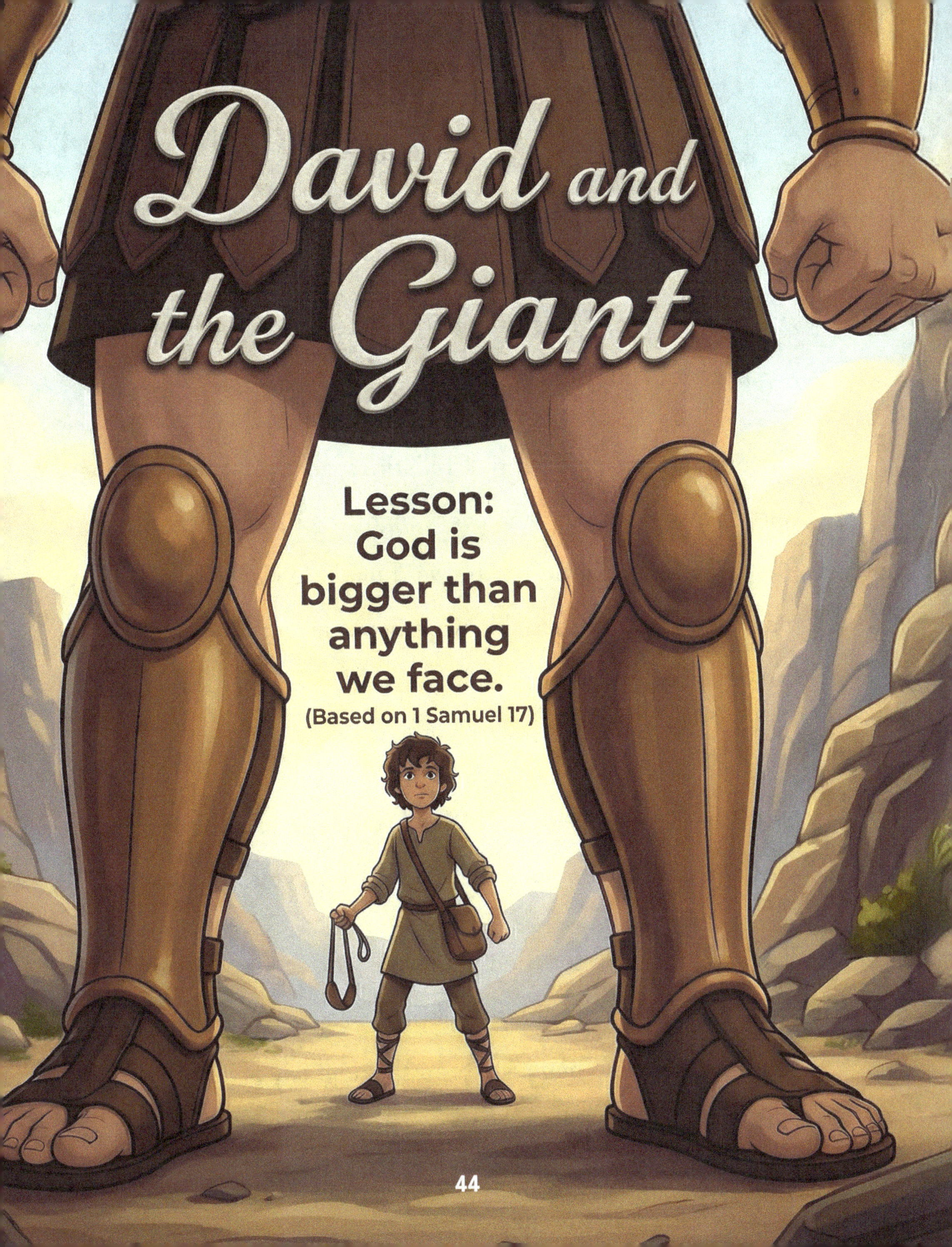

David and the Giant
Lesson: God is bigger than anything we face.
(Based on 1 Samuel 17)
44

A long time ago, God's people, the Israelites, had a big problem. A **giant** problem, to be exact!

The enemy army, called the **Philistines**, sent out their strongest warrior every morning and every night to challenge the Israelites. His name was **Goliath**, and he was huge! He was taller than any man they had ever seen. He wore heavy armor that clanked and shined in the sun. He carried a massive spear, sharp and deadly, with a point as big as a man's hand.

Every day, Goliath shouted, **"Send someone to fight me! If he wins, we will be your servants. But if I win, you will serve us!"**

The Israelites were terrified. No one dared to step forward. Not the strongest soldiers. Not the bravest captains. Not even King Saul, their leader. They just stood shaking, day after day, hoping someone else would be brave enough.

Now, far away from the battlefield, there lived a young boy named **David.** David wasn't a soldier. David was a **simple shepherd** who took care of his family's sheep.

He spent his days playing songs to God on his harp and keeping his flock safe from lions and bears. He had learned to be brave in the fields, but no one thought of him as a warrior.

One day, David's father sent him to the battlefield to bring food to his older brothers, who were soldiers in the Israelite army. When David arrived, he heard Goliath shouting his terrible challenge again. David couldn't believe his ears!

"Why is everyone so afraid?" David asked. **"Don't we have God on our side?"** But the soldiers just shook their heads and turned away. Even King Saul looked worried and afraid.

David stood up straight and said, **"I will fight him!"**

The soldiers laughed out loud. King Saul said, **"You are only a boy. Goliath has been fighting since he was young!"**

But David wasn't scared.

He said, **"When a lion or a bear tried to take my sheep, I chased it down. I fought it off. God kept me safe then, and He will keep me safe now!"**

King Saul finally agreed. He offered David his own heavy armor and a mighty sword. But when David tried to walk in them, he stumbled and wobbled.

"This doesn't fit me," David said, smiling. **"I'll use what I know."**

So David bent down by a bubbling river and picked up **five smooth stones** from the riverbed. He tucked the stones into his leather pouch. He held his simple sling in his hand, just a strip of leather and a heart full of faith in God.

Then David walked onto the battlefield. Goliath roared with laughter when he saw the small boy approaching without a sword or armor.

"Am I a dog, that you come at me with sticks?" he shouted.

But David stood firm. **"You come with a sword and a spear,"** David called out, **"but I come in the name of the Lord! Today, God will win this battle!"**

Goliath charged forward, his armor clanking and his spear raised. David didn't run away. **David ran toward Goliath!**

Quick as a flash, David pulled a stone from his pouch, placed it in his sling, and whirled it around over his head.

Whoosh... whoosh... whoosh...

The stone zipped through the air and struck Goliath, right in the middle of his forehead.

Thud! The giant crashed to the ground face first.

The Philistines gasped in shock. The Israelites cheered with joy!

With God's help, a young boy defeated a mighty warrior with courage, faith, and trust in the Lord. David became a hero that day, not because he was big, or strong, or powerful, but because he trusted in God.

And just like David, when we face scary things, we don't have to be afraid. **God is always bigger than the giants in our lives.**

Little Prayer

Dear God, help me be brave like David. Help me trust that You are bigger than anything I face. Amen.

Jonah and the Fish

Lesson: When we mess up, God still gives us another chance.
(Based on Jonah 1–3)

Once there was a man named **Jonah.** Jonah loved God. Jonah listened to God. **Most of the time.**

One day, God gave Jonah a big job. **"Jonah,"** God said, **"go to the city of Nineveh. Tell the people there to stop doing bad things and turn back to Me."**

But Jonah didn't want to go. He didn't like the people of Nineveh. He thought they were mean and terrible. He didn't think they deserved another chance. He wanted God to punish them instead!

So, Jonah made a choice. **He ran away.**

Instead of going to Nineveh, Jonah boarded a ship sailing in the **opposite direction!** He thought he could hide from God. He thought maybe if he sailed far enough, God would leave him alone.

But you can never really run away from God. **God sees everything. God knows everything. And God still loves us, even when we run.**

While Jonah was on the ship, something happened. The sky grew dark. The wind howled. The waves crashed higher and higher. The sailors were terrified. They threw their cargo overboard to make the ship lighter. They prayed to their gods, hoping for help, but nothing worked.

Finally, they found Jonah fast asleep down below.

"Wake up!" they cried. **"Pray to your God! Maybe He will save us!"**

Jonah knew the truth deep in his heart. **"This is my fault,"** Jonah said. **"I'm running from God. If you throw me into the sea, the storm will stop."**

The sailors didn't want to do it. They tried everything else first. But the storm grew wilder. Finally, they picked Jonah up and tossed him into the raging water.

Splash!

And just like that, the sea grew calm. The sailors stared in amazement. They realized Jonah's God was the real God. The God of all creation!

Meanwhile, Jonah sank deeper and deeper into the sea. The cold water swirled around him. His heart beat fast. He thought it was the end. But God wasn't finished with Jonah yet.

God sent a **giant fish** to save him! **Whoosh!**

The fish swam up through the dark water. It opened its mouth wide. **GULP!** The fish swallowed Jonah whole. But Jonah wasn't hurt, he wasn't crunched. God had provided a safe, strange boat to keep Jonah alive.

Down, down, down Jonah went, safely inside the fish.

He prayed with all his heart. **"God, I'm sorry. Thank You for saving me. I will listen to You. I will do what You ask."**

Jonah's prayer floated up through the sea, through the sky, right into God's loving heart.

God heard Jonah's prayer.

After three days and three nights, the big fish swam close to land. **Blub-blub-blub!** And then—**WHOOSH!**—the fish spit Jonah out onto dry ground!

Soggy and sandy, Jonah sat up. He wiped seaweed from his hair. He took a deep breath of fresh, salty air. And this time, when God said, **"Go to Nineveh,"** Jonah didn't run away. He obeyed.

He walked through the giant city, shouting, **"Stop doing bad things! Turn back to God!"**

The people of Nineveh listened. They stopped hurting each other. They prayed to God with humble hearts. They changed their ways.

And God forgave them. He smiled with joy. He loved them, just like He loved Jonah.

Jonah learned something important that day. **God is a God of second chances for everyone.** When we mess up, God is still there, reaching out to us. He is ready to forgive. Ready to help us start again. Ready to love us, no matter what.

That's how big God's love is. It stretches across the widest oceans. It dives into the deepest seas. It finds us wherever we are and welcomes us home. Always.

Jesus Is Born

Lesson: Jesus came to love you just as you are.
(Based on Luke 2)

Long ago, in a little town called **Nazareth**, there lived a young woman named **Mary**.

Mary loved God with all her heart.

She listened to Him. She trusted Him. She tried to live her life in a way that made God smile.

One day, something amazing happened. An **angel** appeared to Mary! The angel's clothes shone like bright, golden light.

Mary's heart pounded. She felt a little afraid. But the angel said, **"Don't be scared, Mary. God has chosen you for something very special."**

The angel told Mary that she would have **God's own Son!** And His name would be **Jesus.**

Mary was amazed. She didn't understand everything. She had so many questions. But she trusted God.

She bowed her head and said, **"Yes, Lord. I will do whatever You ask."**

At that time, the ruler of the land said that everyone had to go to their hometowns to be counted, like a big family list. So Mary and her soon-to-be husband, **Joseph**, packed their bags and set off on a long, bumpy trip to a town called **Bethlehem.**

Mary rode on a small, steady donkey. Joseph walked beside her, guiding the way. They traveled dusty roads under the hot sun. They climbed rocky hills that made their legs ache. They crossed cold, splashing streams. It was difficult, especially for Mary, who was carrying her precious baby inside her.

When they finally reached Bethlehem, the town was crowded. People were everywhere, talking, laughing, carrying baskets of food, leading donkeys and sheep.

Mary and Joseph looked for a place to stay. They knocked on one door after another.

"No room," said one innkeeper. **"Sorry, we are full,"** said another.

Finally, someone kindly said, "You can stay in the stable, where the animals sleep."

It wasn't fancy. It wasn't clean. But it was safe, and it was warm.

And so, on that quiet night, in a humble stable filled with the soft sounds of animals, **Mary's baby was born.**

Jesus. The Son of God. The Savior of the world. Born in a little stable.

Mary wrapped baby Jesus in soft cloths. She laid Him gently in a manger, a wooden box filled with sweet-smelling hay, normally used for feeding cows and donkeys.

Outside, the night sky was dark, but something wonderful was happening. In fields nearby, shepherds were watching over their sheep. Suddenly, the sky burst into bright, glowing light! An angel appeared to them!

The shepherds trembled with fear, but the angel said, **"Don't be afraid! I bring you good news! Today, in Bethlehem, a Savior has been born to you. He is Christ the Lord!"**

And then, the whole sky filled with angels, a million shining lights singing: **"Glory to God in the highest, and peace on earth to those He loves!"**

The shepherds were amazed.

They hurried to Bethlehem as fast as their feet could carry them. There, just like the angel said, they found Mary, Joseph, and the tiny baby lying in the manger.

The shepherds knelt down. They praised God with all their hearts. They told everyone they met about the amazing baby they had seen.

And Mary? She smiled and treasured all these things in her heart. She knew God's love was shining brighter than all the stars.

That night, something beautiful and powerful happened. **God kept His promise.** He sent His Son, Jesus, to live with us, because He loves us so much.

He came quietly, humbly, as a tiny, helpless baby, so everyone could come close. Jesus came for you, too. Even today, His love shines as brightly as that angel-lit sky.

Whenever you see a Christmas star, or hear a Christmas song, you can remember: **Jesus came because He loves you, forever and always.**

Jesus Feeds the 5,000

Lesson: God can do amazing things with your small gifts.
(Based on John 6)

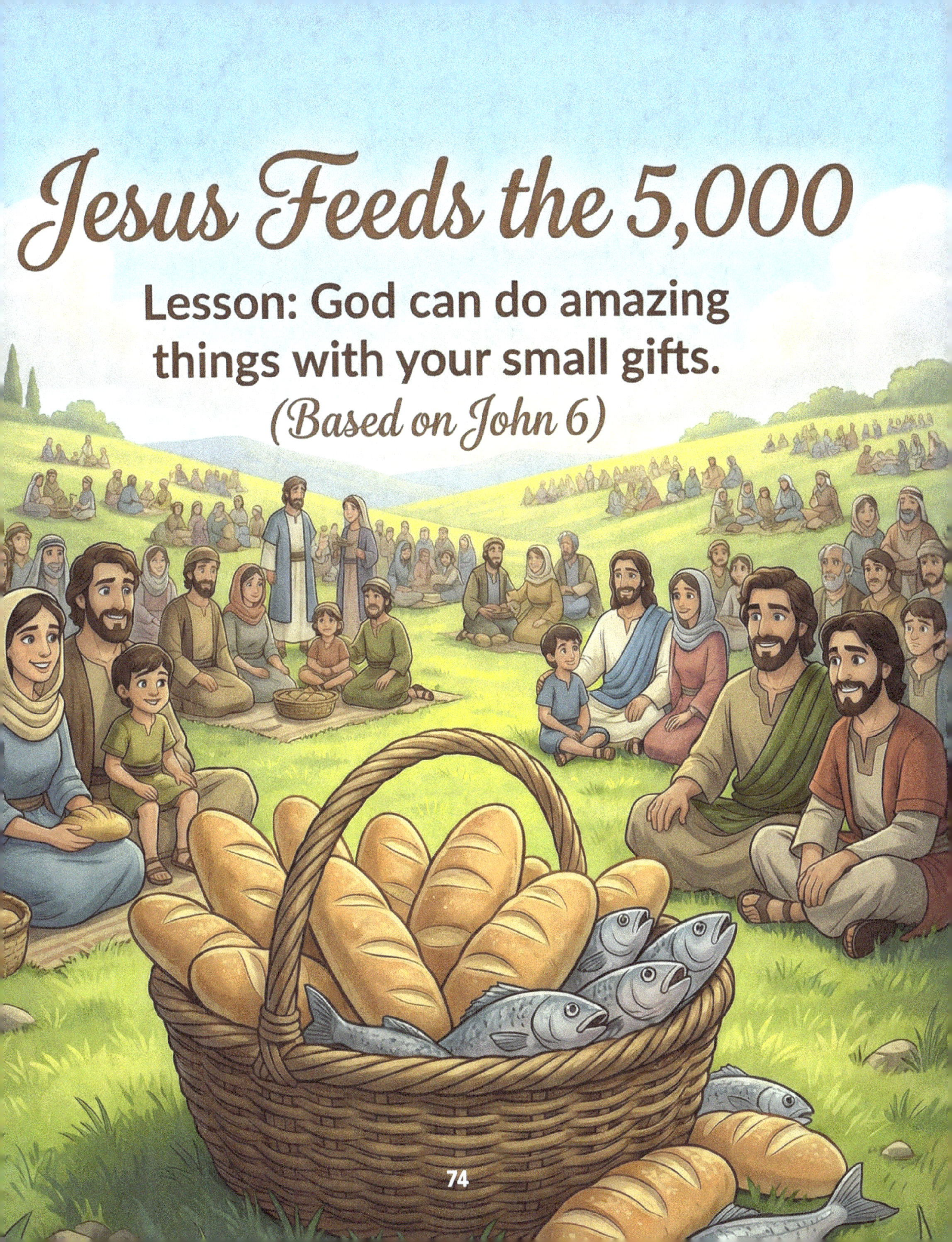

Everywhere Jesus went, people followed Him. They had heard about His amazing miracles. They had listened to His powerful teaching. They had seen His kindness, His joy, and His love. They knew Jesus was someone special, someone sent from God.

One day, **a large crowd** gathered around Jesus. There were thousands of men, women, and children. They wanted to hear His words. They wanted to see His face. They wanted to be close to Him.

Jesus welcomed them all with open arms. He sat down on a grassy hillside and began to teach them about God's love. He spoke about forgiveness, hope, and how to live in a way that made God's heart happy.

The people listened for hours. The sun moved across the sky, bright and warm. The shadows grew longer. The day grew late.

And the people grew **hungry.** Their stomachs rumbled loudly. Children became cranky and tugged at their mothers' robes. Mothers tried to quiet them with soft words and hugs. Fathers looked around, wondering how they could find food in such a lonely place.

Jesus looked at the crowd with kindness. He turned to His disciples and said, **"Where can we buy bread for all these people?"**

The disciples looked at each other, wide-eyed.

Buy bread? For thousands of people?

It would take a huge amount of money, more than any of them had.

One of the disciples, **Andrew**, spoke up. **"Here is a boy,"** Andrew said, **"who has five small loaves of bread and two small fish. But that's not enough for everyone."**

A little boy had offered his small lunch. Just five loaves and two tiny fish, barely enough to feed a few people.

But Jesus smiled. He told the people to sit down in groups on the green grass.

Then He took the little lunch, the five loaves and the two fish, and looked up to heaven. **He thanked God for the food.** He blessed it with love.

Then He broke the bread into pieces. He broke the fish into pieces too. He gave them to His disciples and told them to hand it out to the people.

And then something **amazing** happened. The food didn't run out! Piece after piece, the bread and fish kept coming. The baskets stayed full, no matter how many people took from them.

Everyone ate until they were full. Children wiped crumbs from their mouths and smiled. Tired travelers laughed and shared stories. Fathers passed plates to their families. Mothers fed their little ones, grateful for every bite.

No one was left out. No one was forgotten.

When everyone had eaten all they wanted, Jesus said, **"Collect the leftover food, so none of it gets thrown away."**

The disciples went out with their baskets. And guess what? They filled **twelve whole baskets** with leftover bread and fish! From one little lunch, God had fed over 5,000 people!

The people were amazed. They looked at each other with wide eyes and joyful hearts. They knew something special had happened. They knew that with Jesus, even the smallest gifts could turn into something wonderful.

Jesus had taken something small and made it **more than enough.**
That's what God does. When we give Him what we have, even if it
seems small, He can use it to do amazing things.

You don't have to be the strongest. You don't have to be the
smartest. You don't have to be the richest. You just have to bring
your willing, loving heart and share what you have. Because in
God's hands, even a little becomes **a lot.**

And when you give with love, you are part of God's beautiful
miracle too.

Little Prayer

Dear God, help me share what I have with You and others. I know You can do big things with my little gifts. Amen.

Jesus Walks on Water
Lesson: When we look to Jesus, we don't sink.
(Based on Matthew 14)

After a long day of teaching and helping people, Jesus told His disciples, **"Get in the boat and go across the lake. I'll catch up with you later."**

The disciples did just as Jesus said. They climbed into a wooden boat and set sail across the wide, dark lake. The sun went down. The sky turned deep purple and then black. The stars twinkled far above them.

The wind picked up. The water grew choppy. Waves started to rock the boat back and forth.

The disciples rowed hard against the wind. They rowed and rowed,
but the boat didn't seem to move far. It was the middle of the night.
They were cold. They were tired. Their arms ached from rowing.

And they were starting to feel a little afraid.

Where was Jesus? Why hadn't He come with them?

Meanwhile, Jesus had gone up onto a mountain to pray by Himself. He talked to His Father, God. He thanked Him. He listened quietly in the stillness. But even far away, Jesus knew His friends needed Him.

So, Jesus did something **amazing.** He didn't find another boat. He didn't shout across the waves. Instead, He simply **walked right onto the water!**

Step after step, Jesus moved across the waves, not sinking, not splashing, just calmly walking, as if the water were a smooth stone path. The wind blew His robe around Him. The waves rolled and sloshed at His feet. But Jesus walked steadily, full of peace and power.

When the disciples saw someone walking toward them on the water, they were terrified!

"It's a ghost!" they cried out.

They huddled together, shivering from both cold and fear. Their hearts raced. Their hands trembled.

But then they heard a familiar voice, strong and kind: **"Take courage! It's Me. Don't be afraid!"**

It was Jesus!

Peter, one of the boldest disciples, called out: **"Lord, if it's really You, tell me to come to You on the water!"**

Jesus smiled and said one word: **"Come."**

Peter took a deep breath. He swung one leg over the side of the boat. Then the other. And he stood, not sinking, on top of the water! One step. Then another. Peter was walking on water too, just like Jesus!

The wind whipped around him. The waves splashed at his ankles. But as long as Peter kept his eyes on Jesus, he stayed steady. His heart was brave. His feet were sure.

But then Peter noticed the wind roaring in his ears. He saw the dark waves swirling under his feet. He stopped looking at Jesus. He started looking at the storm.

Fear crept into his heart. And then he began to sink!

"Lord, save me!" Peter cried, reaching out his hand.

Immediately, Jesus reached out too. He grabbed Peter firmly and pulled him up. Jesus looked at Peter with love and said gently: **"You have little faith. Why did you doubt?"**

They climbed back into the boat together. And as soon as Jesus stepped inside, the wind died down. The waves became still. The sea grew quiet. The stars reflected softly on the calm water.

The disciples stared at Jesus with wide eyes. They had never seen anyone do what Jesus had done. They fell to their knees and worshiped Him, saying: **"You really are God's Son!"**

That night, the disciples learned something important. When storms come, the safest thing we can do is keep our eyes on Jesus. When we focus on Him, we stand strong, even when everything around us feels scary.

When we concentrate on fear, we start to sink. But even when we sink, Jesus is right there. He reaches out His hand. He catches us. He pulls us close. He will never let us go. No matter how big the waves are, no matter how strong the winds blow, **Jesus is always stronger.** And with Him, we are never truly afraid.

Little Prayer

Dear Jesus, help me keep my eyes on You, even when life feels scary. Thank You for always reaching out to catch me. Amen.

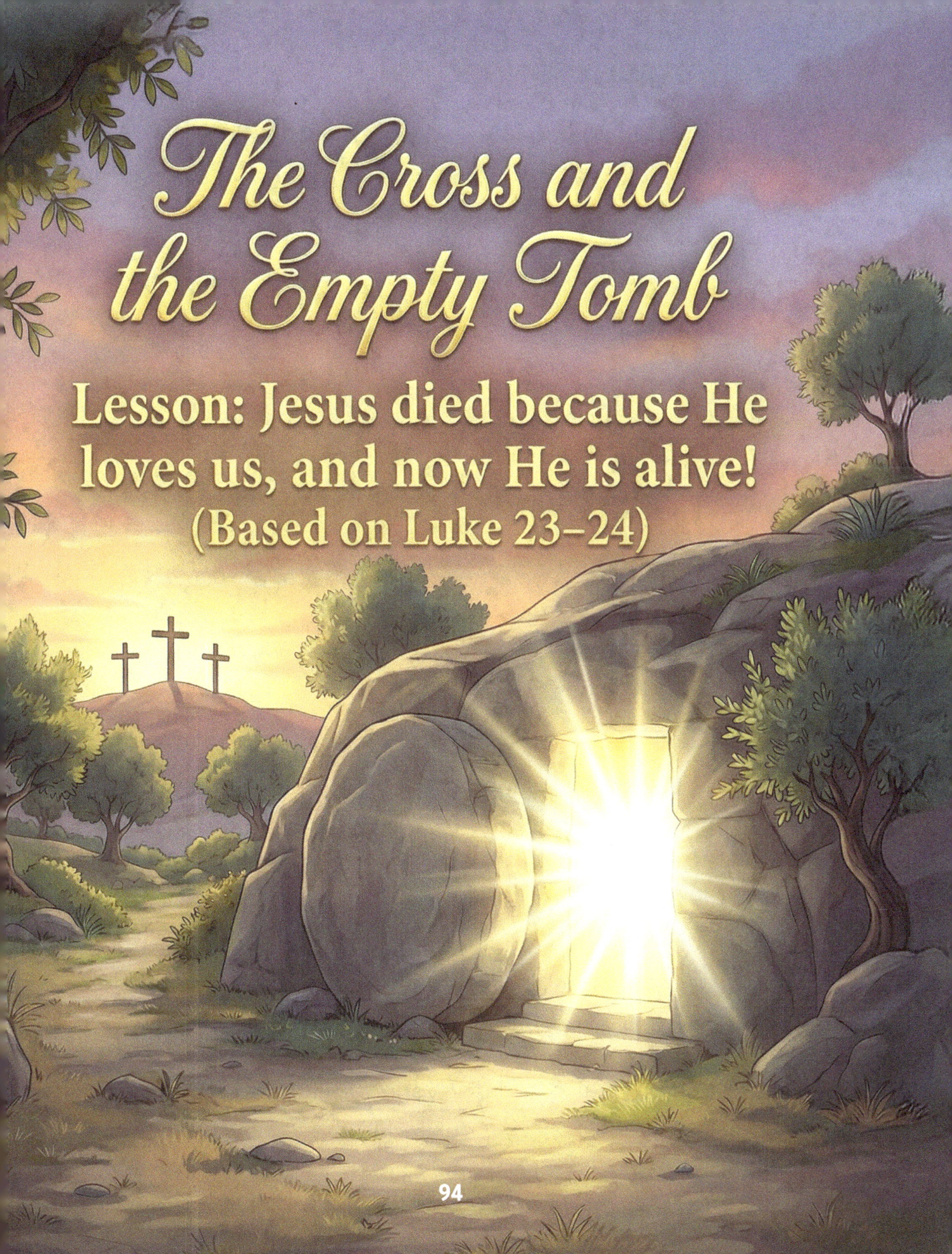

The Cross and the Empty Tomb
Lesson: Jesus died because He loves us, and now He is alive!
(Based on Luke 23–24)

Jesus had done many wonderful things. He healed the sick. He fed the hungry. He loved the lonely. He taught everyone about **God's amazing love.**

Everywhere Jesus went, crowds gathered to listen to His words. Children sat on His lap. Mothers and fathers brought their families to hear Him. He welcomed everyone with kindness and joy.

But not everyone liked what Jesus was doing. Some leaders were jealous. They didn't want Jesus to be King. They didn't understand that His Kingdom was all about love, not power. They were afraid of losing their important places.

One sad day, soldiers came to take Jesus away. They hurt Him badly. They made fun of Him, laughing cruelly. They twisted sharp thorns into a painful crown and pressed it onto His head. They forced Jesus to carry a heavy wooden cross through the crowded streets.

The people who loved Jesus cried.

They didn't understand why this was happening. They had believed He was the Savior. Now they watched Him stumble and fall.

Jesus was taken to a hill called **Golgotha**, which means "The Place of the Skull." The soldiers nailed Him to the cross. Thick, heavy nails pinned His hands and feet to the wood. It was a terrible, painful way to die.

But even as He hung on the cross, Jesus showed love. He prayed out loud, **"Father, please forgive them. They don't understand what they're doing."**

The sky grew dark, even though it was the middle of the day. The earth shook beneath everyone's feet. And when it was finished, **Jesus bowed His head and died.**

His friends were heartbroken. Their hearts felt crushed with sadness.

They carefully took His body down from the cross. They wrapped Him gently in **linen cloths**, like a soft blanket. They placed Him in a tomb. A big, heavy stone was rolled in front of the opening. The door was shut.

It seemed like the end. The whole world felt heavy, dark, and sad. But the story wasn't over.

God's plan was just getting started. Three days later, early in the morning, some women who loved Jesus went to visit the tomb. They carried spices and oils to honor Him. Their hearts were heavy with sorrow.

But when they arrived, they were shocked! The stone had been rolled away! The tomb was **empty!** They didn't know what to think. Had someone taken Jesus's body? Where had He gone?

Suddenly, two angels appeared beside them, shining bright like lightning! The women were frightened and bowed low.

But the angels said, **"Why do you look for the living among the dead? Jesus isn't here, He's alive again!"**

The women's hearts raced with joy! They ran as fast as they could to tell the disciples the good news.

At first, the disciples didn't believe them. But soon, they saw for themselves. Jesus appeared to them **alive!** He walked with them along the road. He talked with them about God's promises. He even shared a meal with them, breaking bread just like He had before.

Jesus had conquered death! He had defeated sin! He had made a way for everyone, for you and for me, to be close to God forever.

That sad day at the cross was not the end. It was the beginning of something beautiful. Because of Jesus, we can live with hope, joy, and love every single day.

When we see a cross, we remember His great love for us. When we celebrate Easter, we remember His incredible victory. And when we feel sad, afraid, or alone, we can remember **Jesus is alive!**

He will never leave us. He will never stop loving us. He promises to be with us always, from now until forever. That is the best news ever! And because of Jesus, we can have a forever friendship with God.

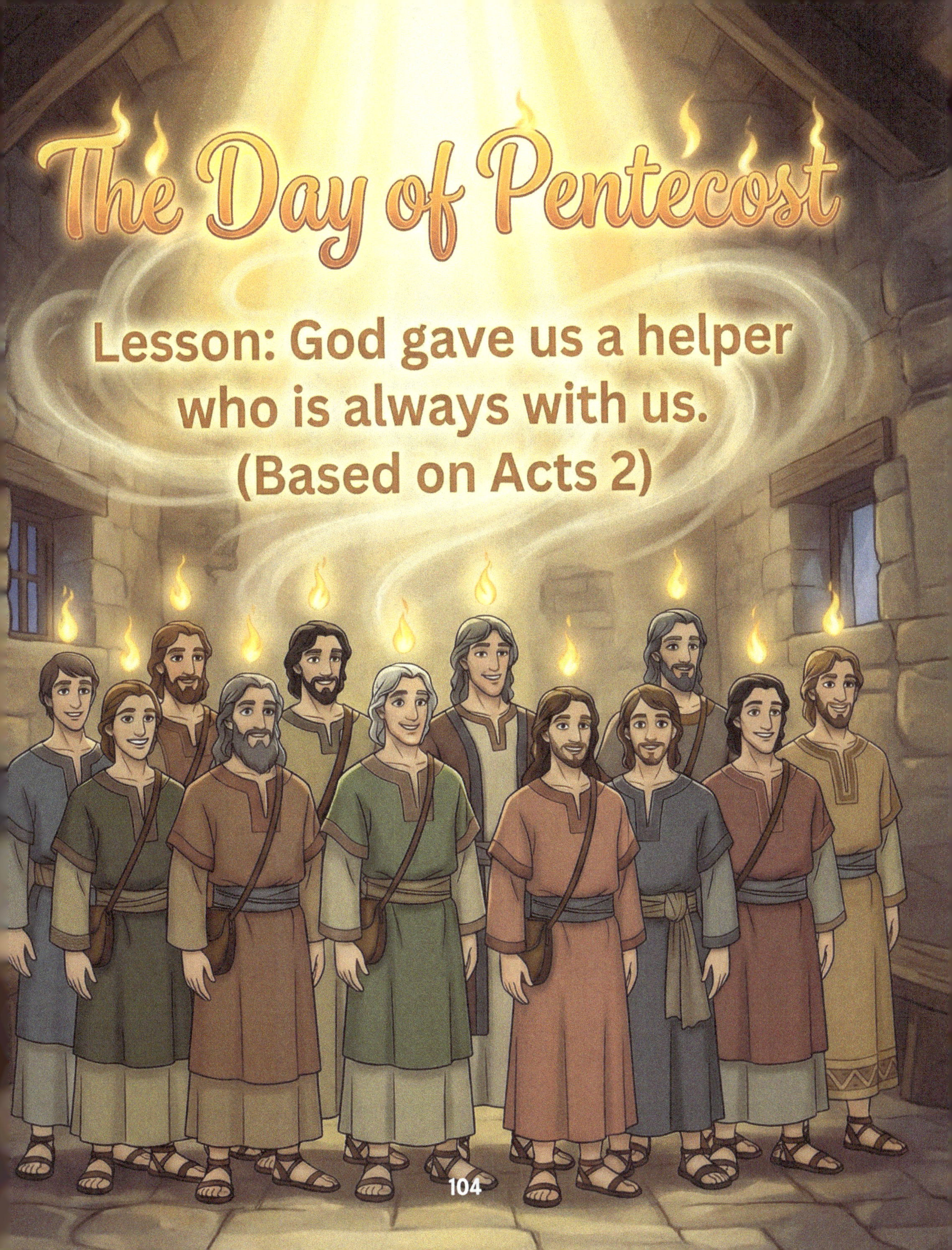

The Day of Pentecost
Lesson: God gave us a helper who is always with us.
(Based on Acts 2)

After Jesus rose from the dead, He spent precious time with His disciples. He walked with them. He talked with them. He ate meals with them and explained more about God's Kingdom, a Kingdom filled with love, hope, and eternal life.

Jesus made a special promise. He said, **"Soon, you will receive power from God. I will send you a helper—the Holy Spirit."**

The disciples listened carefully. They didn't know exactly what the Holy Spirit would be like, but they trusted Jesus.

Then, one day, Jesus led His friends outside the city. He lifted His hands, blessed them, and then something amazing happened. **Jesus rose right up into the clouds!** He floated higher and higher until they couldn't see Him anymore.

The disciples stood there staring at the sky, amazed and a little unsure. **What would happen next?**

Two angels appeared beside them and said, **"Why are you looking up into the sky? Jesus will come back one day, just like you saw Him leave!"**

Jesus had told them to wait, to stay in **Jerusalem** until the special gift arrived. So, they waited.

They gathered together in a big upstairs room. They prayed. They sang songs. They remembered everything Jesus had taught them. And they waited some more. They didn't know exactly when the promise would come.

But they trusted God.

One day, during a special Jewish festival called Pentecost, the disciples were all together.

Suddenly, without warning, something amazing happened! **Whoooosh!** A sound like a mighty rushing wind filled the whole house! It wasn't like any wind they had ever felt. It didn't knock anything over or blow things around. But it filled the air with the feeling of **power** and **energy!**

Then, small flames of fire appeared over each disciple's head! But the flames didn't burn them. They didn't hurt them. It was something **wonderful.** It was the Holy Spirit!

Just as Jesus promised, **God's Spirit** came to live inside them!

The disciples felt full of courage, joy, and strength. They started speaking in many languages so people from all over the world could understand! It was incredible!

Outside, a huge crowd gathered from **all over the world.** They heard the strange noise and the different languages. They were confused, but curious.

"What's happening?" they asked. **"How can we hear them in our own language?"**

Some people laughed, **"They must have had too much wine!"**

But Peter, filled with boldness from the Holy Spirit, stood up strong. He said, **"No! We are not drunk! This is the power of God you are seeing! This is what Jesus promised!"**

Peter told the people about Jesus, how He lived, how He died, and how He rose again. He explained that Jesus had sent the Holy Spirit so that everyone who believed could have God living with them, always.

When the people heard Peter's message, their hearts were stirred. They felt something deep inside, a longing to be close to God. They asked, **"What should we do?"**

Peter answered, **"Turn away from your wrong choices. Be baptized. Follow Jesus. And you will receive the gift of the Holy Spirit too!"**

That day, an amazing thing happened. **3,000 people** believed in Jesus! They were baptized, and they became part of the first church.

From that day forward, the disciples went everywhere telling people about Jesus. They were filled with the Holy Spirit, filled with courage, filled with love, filled with the truth of God.

And the Holy Spirit didn't stop with them. Even today, when we choose to follow Jesus, we receive that same amazing gift. **The Holy Spirit lives inside us—helping us love others, giving us strength, guiding us, comforting us.**

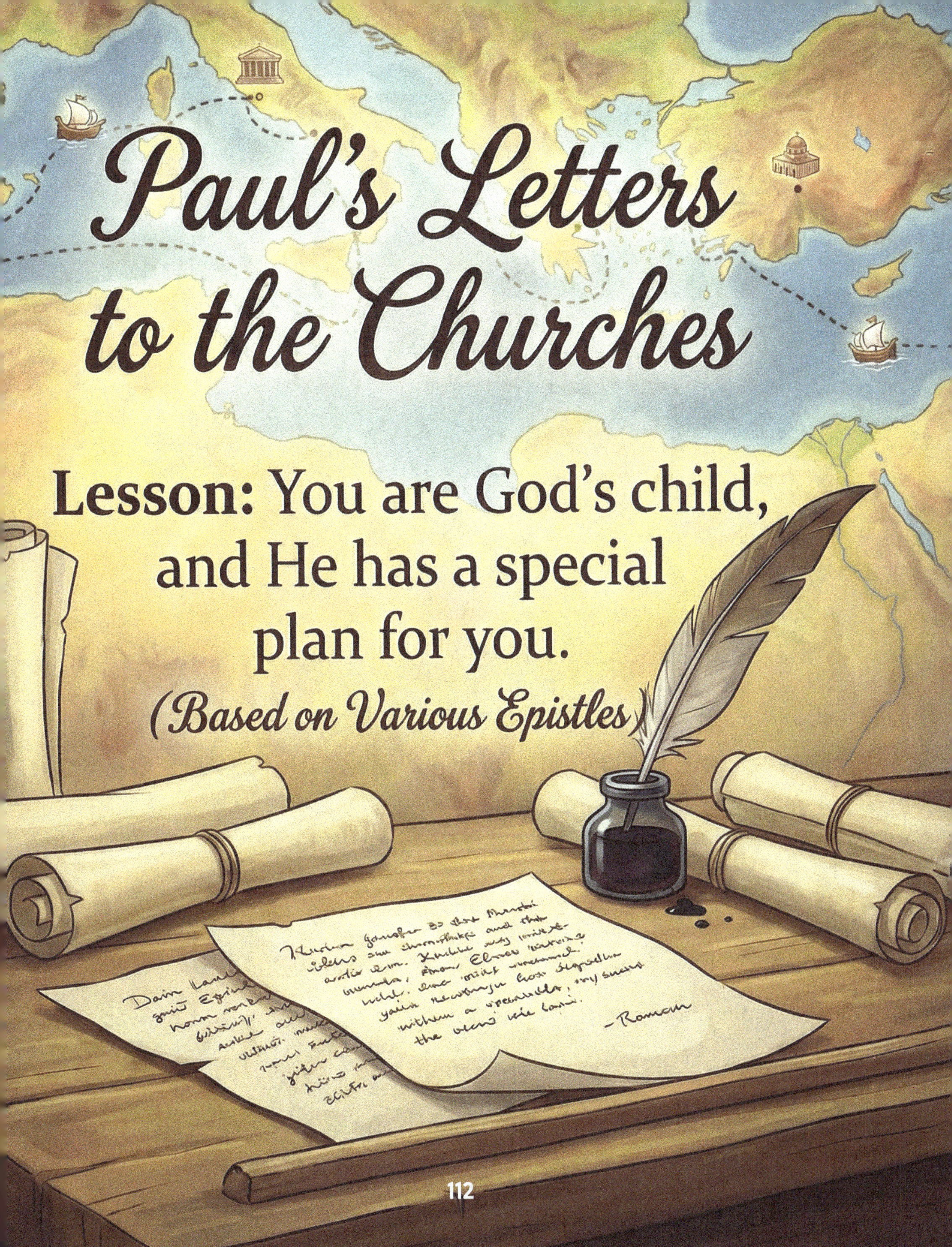

Paul's Letters to the Churches

Lesson: You are God's child, and He has a special plan for you.

(Based on Various Epistles)

After Jesus went back to Heaven, His followers had a big, important job to do. They needed to tell the whole world about Jesus—about His love, His forgiveness, and the hope He gives to everyone who believes.

One man named **Paul** took that job seriously. But Paul didn't always follow Jesus. At first, Paul tried to stop people from believing. He thought he was doing the right thing, but he was wrong. He even chased after people who loved Jesus and tried to scare them. He wanted to shut down the good news.

But everything changed one amazing day when Paul met Jesus on the road to **Damascus.** A bright, blinding light shone down from Heaven, and Paul fell to the ground.

He heard a powerful voice say: **"Paul, why are you hurting Me?"**

It was Jesus, speaking directly to him! From that moment, Paul's heart was brand new. He realized Jesus really was the Son of God, the Savior he had been fighting against without even knowing it.

Paul's whole life turned around. Instead of chasing after believers to stop them, he became one of Jesus's biggest helpers!

Paul traveled to cities far and wide. He crossed hot deserts with blistering winds. He sailed across stormy seas. He walked for days and days through bright sun and dark nights.

Everywhere he went, Paul shared the good news about Jesus. He taught people about God's love. He started new churches, places where people could gather together to worship, pray, sing, and grow in faith. He made many new friends who loved Jesus too.

But Paul couldn't be everywhere at once. He couldn't stay with every church and every friend. So Paul wrote letters, lots and lots of letters!

He wrote to churches in places like **Rome, Corinth, Galatia**, and **Ephesus.** He wrote to his young friends like **Timothy** and **Titus**, giving them advice and encouragement.

He even wrote letters while he was sitting in dark, cold prison cells!

Paul's letters were filled with encouragement, wisdom, and hope. He reminded people that **God loves them no matter what.** They are saved by grace, not by being perfect. **They are part of God's big forever family. They have a special purpose to show God's love to others.**

In one letter, Paul wrote: **"Nothing can separate us from God's love: not trouble, not sadness, not anything at all!"**

In another, he said: **"Put on the full armor of God - truth, righteousness, peace, faith, salvation, and God's Word - so you can stand strong every single day."**

Paul's letters became treasures. They weren't just for the people back then. They are for us today too!

When we feel lonely, God's Word reminds us: **"You are never alone."** When we feel weak, God's Word says: **"You are strong through Jesus."** When we feel unsure, scared, or small, God's Word tells us: **"You are chosen. You are loved. You are important."**

Paul wanted everyone to know: If you believe in Jesus, you are part of God's forever family. You are a shining light in a dark world. You are a masterpiece, created with a wonderful plan and purpose.

Sometimes life is hard. Sometimes we feel too small or not good enough. But God's promises are always bigger than any problem we face.

And through Paul's letters, God is still speaking today, encouraging you, guiding you, and cheering you on. It's almost like God has written a special letter just for **you.**

A letter that says: **"I love you. I am with you. I have good plans for your life."**

All you have to do is open your heart and listen. Because God's Word is His forever love letter to your heart every single day.

Little Prayer

Dear God, thank You for Your Word. Help me to listen to it, trust it, and live for You every day. Amen.

God's Story and Yours

You've just traveled through some of the most
wonderful stories ever told. Stories of creation,
courage, forgiveness, miracles, and love.
Stories of people, just like you, who trusted God,
even when life was hard. Stories that show us
that God is always good, always near, and always
working for our good.

But guess what? The story isn't over.
God's story keeps going, and you are part of it!
Every moment, you are held in God's great love.
No matter where you go, no matter what happens,
remember this: God made you. God loves you.
And God has a beautiful plan for your life.
So keep listening. Keep trusting. Keep shining bright.
The adventure with God is just getting started,
and it's the best adventure of all!

Keep the Conversation Going!

Download Your Free 'Little Hearts' Companion Pack

Thank you for sharing these stories with your little ones. We believe that the best part of a Bible story isn't just the reading— it's the connection that happens afterward. To help you bridge the gap between storytime and daily life, we've created a special collection of printable resources for your family.

- **Scripture Memory Cards:** 10 beautifully designed cards to help your child carry God's Word in their heart throughout the day. Perfect for the fridge, the car, or bedside.

- **The "Table Talk" Discussion Guide:** Simple, thoughtful questions for every story in this book. These prompts are designed to spark big conversations and help children see how God is working in their own lives.

- **"My Daily Conversation" Prayer Journal:** A gentle, two-page template that teaches children the habit of prayer through gratitude, reflection, and big dreams.

These resources are designed to turn five minutes of reading into a lifetime of faith. They are quick to print, easy to use, and crafted to help your child feel confident in God's love.

Scan the QR code below to download your free Activity Pack instantly!